Marriage: The Journey "How Do You Handle Your Baggage?"

By

Stephen A. Butterfield, Sr.

Stephen A. Butterfield, Sr.

MARRIAGE THE JOURNEY®.

Copyright © 2020 by Stephen Butterfield, Sr.

Published by BMW Press

Lithonia, GA 30058

All rights reserved. *No portion of this book may be reproduced or transmitted in any form or by and means electronic or mechanical, including photocopying without permission in writing from the publisher.*

Unless otherwise indicated, all scripture quotations are taken from the King James Version® and The Messenger Bible®

All emphasis in Scripture quotation has been added by the author

Printed in the United States of America

Table of Contents

Introduction
Acknowledgments
Foreword by Archbishop Ruth W. Smith

Introduction   13

PART ONE
Marriage

1 Marriage: The Definition   31

PART TWO
Preparation for Marriage

2 Pre-Marital Counseling   50

PART THREE
Naked and Exposed

3 Who Are You, Really?   59
4 Family Traits: Traditions   65
5 Love Languages   70
6 Beliefs: Firmly Held Convictions   83
7 Habits: Learned Behavior   90
8 Unresolved Issues   93

PART FOUR
Children

9 Children   100

PART FIVE
Finances

10 Finances   105

PART SIX
Mid-Life Crisis

11	Mid-Life Crisis & Menopause	111

PART SEVEN
Baggage Handler
Intimacy

12	Identify the Baggage	114
13	Step 1: Encounter	119
14	Step 2: Submission	126
15	Step 3: Transformation	142
16	Step 4: Oneness	147

PART EIGHT
Annual Marital Checkup

17	Annual Marital Check-Up	151
	About the Author	155

In Loving memory
Of Pearl Winifred Augusta Butterfield

On December 9th, 1925 a beautiful baby girl was born to the late Percy James Sturrup and the late Zilpha "Hattie" Sturrup who resided in Georgetown, Exuma. From that day everyone knew that this baby girl was someone special. She was the seventh child out of eleven, and she was named Pearl Winifred Augusta.

She lived her life as an example, not only to her family, but to the many people that she met. A virtuous woman, a priceless gem, a strong provider, and spiritual mother, the list could go on and on.

She was a piano player and amazed many with her high-pitched soprano voice. She played many different roles in the church such as: Sunday School Superintendent and Teacher, Treasurer of the Ladies Ministry (for many years) and also Choir Director. This woman of God was a friend to the lonely, a mother to many, a counselor to the confused and meal ticket for the hungry.

Mother Pearl heard the long-awaited call of "Come home my child" at 3:05 p.m. on the Sunday afternoon of September 9th, 2012.

Stephen A. Butterfield, Sr.

Acknowledgements

First, I would like to thank the Lord, Jesus the Christ, for His grace and love toward me, which helps me to abound more and more. Thank you, God, for entrusting me with this revelation that will revolutionize relationships and marriages worldwide, especially in the body of Christ. I pray that this revelation is communicated so that the intended message is received, exercised, and yes, lived out.

Next, I thank God for my wife, Ann Pearl Butterfield, who I love very much, and who is my inspiration. Thank you for supporting me and being my number one fan.

Next, I thank God for my mother, Pearl Butterfield, who has lived the BIBLE before me and inspired me to live for and serve the King of Kings, Jesus. She went to be with the Lord on September 5, 2012. I thank God for my dad, Jack Butterfield, who passed away on March 10, 2010. He blessed me with his charm and tender heart, may they both rest in peace.

Next, I thank God for my sister, Sharon Pollard, who has been an awesome caregiver for my mom and dad. She is also the reason why I dress like I do! As children, she would not allow me to go outside the house with my clothes not matching, and pressed.

Next, I thank God for our six adult children and their spouses: Lashawn, Stephanie, Stephen, Jr. (Lakeitras), Darryl (Lanessa), David (Tina), and Tamekia. Also, I thank God for our 15 grandchildren: Nathan, Jasmine, Xavier, Danila, LaMarkus, Myran, Luka, Gloria, Shanta,

Rachael, Ramiah, Malcolm, Ashanti, Sariah and RaKiya and our 2 great-grandsons: Rashad and Damien.

I thank God for the late and great, Archbishop Jimmie Lee Smith who provoked a paradigm shift in my view of God's love for humanity and our true purpose in the Kingdom of God. Lastly, I also thank God for Bishop Ruth W. Smith who inspires me every day with her courage to face the many challenges that life sends her. She may never know how she inspired me to return to school after 25 years to earn my Master's Degree in Business Administration in 2010 and then my Masters of Psychology in Counseling in 2016.

Foreword

Archbishop Ruth W. Smith
Light of the World Christian Tabernacle

Author Stephen Butterfield has captured some critical insight concerning marriage. Many times, God teaches us as much through our failures, as our success. I agree that Romans 8:28 is always at work in the lives of the Children of God!

I love his perspective on handling the baggage from prior relationships. It is always a joy to hear the testimony of those who are married to their high school sweethearts. However, this book reaches across the lines to those who do not have that testimony!

This is a must read for singles to get wisdom, as well as, for those who are married who want help staying the course and certainly for those who have attained longevity in marriage!

Every once in a while, a book comes along that really changes your life. Every once in a while, an author is so changed by their own experiences that they have such a passion to transparently share their triumphs, travailing struggles, and successes. This book fits that profile of a once in a while book that has come along and strategically seeded you with encouragement, insight, and instruction all at the same time.

Having personally experienced many of the situations and circumstances that Stephen deals with in this book, I have gained a greater appreciation for my own experiences and gained some much-needed wisdom to help me avoid others. Stephen helps you to see the value in transparency and that there is purpose in your pain.

Preface

I really believe that God has given me great revelation concerning relationships and marriage. If you are tired of just going through the motions in your marriage, I declare and decree that the principles written in this book will help to have the marriage God intended for you!

As I searched for answers concerning my own failed marriages, I began to journal my thoughts, and answers to my prayers. I soon noticed that couples in crisis were asking for my help and when I shared the things that I wrote in my journal, I noticed that their relationships and marriage improved. It was then that I realized that my experiences were for a greater purpose than merely the personal understanding that I had received. God allowed me to go through those circumstances so that I could edify, educate and empower couples around the world to conquer those same issues in their marriages.

Before moving forward with the remainder of this book, please know that I have since repented for breaking my vows before God as well as to my ex-wives and received both theirs and God's forgiveness. I would also like to offer the body of Christ my humblest apologies for adding to the staggering statistics of divorce in the church and bringing reproach to Christians. I spent years trying to forgive myself until I heard a clear word from God saying, "Sinners repent, and I forgive them," so I immediately repented. Now, I thank you in advance for your forgiveness.

Please read this book with an open mind and I hope that you will receive revelation on the everyday things which you may have never considered vital to your marriage. I also hope that you will receive knowledge that will give you the recipe for a successful marriage. May you receive understanding, which is the comprehension of the recipe for a successful marriage. And finally, my hope is that you will use wisdom, which is the use and application of the principles for a successful marriage in this book. You will learn to understand yourself, your spouse, your relationships and your marriage.

My prayer for you is that as you read this book that you will understand the changes that will or may occur during the journey of marriage and make the necessary changes and adjustments when needed. Please be brutally honest and reveal the REAL you to your spouse/fiancée. Yes, get naked. Invest your time and energy into your relationship. Dare to get better day by day. Pursue PEACE with everything you have. Jesus said that He came that we may have life and life in abundance. He meant health, wealth and happiness (JOY). We should not settle for mediocrity in our marriages. Marriage should be whole and complete.

I wish you peace, **SHALOM.**

Introduction

Introduction

I feel obligated to tell you my story, and how God gave me a better understanding and revelation on what it takes to have a healthy marriage.

I am Stephen Alexander Butterfield, Sr., Pearl Butterfield's baby boy and Jack Butterfield's oldest son. I have two younger brothers, and one sister who is older than myself. My mother also helped to raise one of my cousins, who I also consider my big sister. We were born and raised with godly principles and good morals in Nassau, Bahamas. My father left us when I was four months old, so my mother became a single parent who tried to fill the role of two parents. My mother's parenting style was nothing short of militant. She woke us up every morning at 6 am, rain or shine, whether we had school or not. Our regiment during the school year involved getting up at 6 am with devotion, brushing our teeth, bathing, getting dressed, eating breakfast and then off to school we would go. After school we would have a snack, do our homework and chores, and have playtime; all in that order. My mother lived according to the Bible before us, and many called her *too strict*. We had devotion every Sunday morning and attended church every time the doors were opened. She wasn't an affectionate person, so there was no kissing and hugging going on, but we knew she loved us. Years later, after my first divorce, I lived with my mother and it was during that time that we shared many hugs and kisses. I would kiss her every day and she loved it. While my siblings and I were growing up, my mother provided for all of us and gave us whatever we needed. We never went without. To me, she was the epitome of perseverance. As a single parent during the 50s and 60s, she purchased a plot of land and built a home from the ground up. She didn't have a "Sugar Daddy" and didn't have any help from my Father.

I had to overcome many odds while growing up including having an iron deficiency and bronchitis. My mother thought that I would not be able to play any type of sports or participate in any extracurricular activities at school. In order to stay healthy, I had to eat beets and liver, drink beet juice, and get B_{12} shots every other weekend by Nurse King. I decided that life had to be about more than that.

I saw persistency in my mother, as a single parent working and achieving her goals. She inspired me to do things that I shouldn't be able to do. So, I played on all the sports teams at school, played trumpet in my high school band, sang in the school choir, and formed and lead a gospel singing group at 13 years old. Failure was never an option in our house. We lived by the verses in Proverbs that said, *"Whether a task big or small, do it well or not at all"* and *"Once a task has begun, never leave until it's done"*.

As a youth, the best way I thought that I could show my gratitude to my mom was by staying out of trouble and excelling in school. In the process, I graduated one year early because I was able to skip the 11th grade. After graduating high school, I went on to attend Borough of Manhattan Community College in New York. A couple of years later, I moved to Miami with my Mom, and met and married my first wife, Sharon. She shared the same name as my sister, God rest her soul.

We were married for 19 years and produced four beautiful children who gave us nine adorable grandchildren. In retrospect, I realize that marriage without spiritual guidance is like walking in a mine field thinking that it is a playground or park. I made some mistakes in my marriage by not understanding marriage, and my spouse. I thought that if I showed love to my spouse and be romantic like I read in the Harold Robbins' books that everything would be great. While dating, I brought her flowers, opened doors for her, and treated her the way I thought a lady should be treated. She told me that she never had anyone to give her flowers or treat her special before, and she was so happy. Our first child was born a year later. We decided she would stay home with our child while I worked and attended college. Things were going great and we were admired by other couples.

After five years of marriage, we had four children. Then, she began to express her unhappiness. She began to complain about not having enough time to do things for our children and the house. To make her happy, I would fix my girls' hair, iron the children's clothes, bathe them, and dress them when we would go out. After doing these things, she was still unhappy, but I enjoyed the time I spent taking care of my children. I washed, ironed, cleaned, cooked, repaired our car, did house repairs, took the children to the park, prepared birthday surprises, and planned trips. It still didn't result in her being happy.

Doing "acts of service" was my love language toward her, but my wife didn't do personal things for me. She refused to iron my clothes for me. I felt unappreciated and also unloved. I was well liked and respected on my job, in the community, in the church, and everywhere I went; but not at home. When I look back, we were just roommates, who were co-parenting. At that time, my wife told me that I was not good enough for her and that she could do a whole lot better. These words and her contentious attitude toward me were destroying my feelings for her. I continued to do whatever I thought would change her mind about me and love me again.

After years of living like this, I became very depressed and suicidal. The thought of divorce was horrifying. My father was divorced several times and the thought that I was becoming just like my father, a divorced man, was terrifying. I vividly remember spending hours in the night looking for ways to fix our marriage, with no success. I lived with the knowledge of being married to someone who felt that I wasn't good enough. This obliterated my self-esteem because, as a child, I sought the approval of my mother. I decided to stay in the marriage for the benefit of the children and to keep my vows that I made before God and the wedding guests. Our lives were filled with arguments, no sex, no affection and no love. Years without consummation will cause your spirits to disconnect. This is what happened to us.

I fell into a deep depression. I medicated myself and found solace with community activities, school mentoring and coaching. After years of fighting the urge to murder my family and myself, I did the thing that I regret the most. I left and filed for divorce. I remember so vividly how many nights that I sat on the side our bed fighting the thoughts and the spirit of murder and suicide. During those times there would be news reports about men committing murder and suicide. I knew the devil wanted to kill me, but I am still here today to tell my story. I felt that the safest thing to do was to leave my toxic marriage. I regret it only because of the affect it had on my children. I didn't want to be married to someone who did not want me. My heart bled as my baby girl begged me not to leave. It bothers me even as I write this because, I never wanted to leave my children, like my Dad left me.

In 2007, I went to Florida with my youngest son and his family to spend Christmas with the rest of the family. We stayed with my ex-wife. The morning after our arrival, I took her to breakfast with Jasmine our granddaughter. We apologized and forgave each other for our mistakes that we made during our marriage. She actually admitted that someone on her job convinced her that she could do better than me, so she began complaining about everything with the hope that I would leave. During that time, she would do things to provoke me to leave so that she could find a better husband. She said that after dating a guy name Henry, she realized that she had a great husband in me. She promised that she would tell our children after Christmas in 2007. She never did tell them, and she has since passed away.

My second marriage lasted seven years and produced no children (Thank God). I had purposed in my heart that this marriage would be different. This time around, I would be more understanding and caring. So, I serenaded this wife, ran her a bubble bath, chilled the apple cider and sat it beside the tub with soft music playing in the background. I had roses delivered to her regularly. I mailed romantic cards to the house "just because". I rolled and set her hair every weekend. I gave and received full body rubs with lotion almost every day. I opened every door for her, planned and took romantic trips, bought gifts, did most of the cooking, helped with house cleaning, took care of all the cars and made sure they were clean and full of gas. Everything seemed great, until about two years later. My wife began complaining about everything—even the color of the roses that I gave her!

I thought I knew what a woman wanted as far as romance because my big sister Sandra and I read most of Harold Robbins' romance novels when we were growing up. I had also inherited a flair for the ladies from my Dad, which meant I knew how to treat the ladies. So, I began doing some soul searching. The thought of having the generational curse of having multiple marriages was haunting me, which was why I bent over backwards to make this marriage work. Every time I thought about giving up on my marriages, I heard a voice saying, ***"You are just like your father."*** I was determined to learn the secret to having a successful marriage and pass it on to my children.

I began my search with the books and tapes of Godly men and women who taught of healthy marriages and relationships. As I searched, I studied many materials such as Dr. Gary Coleman's, *"The Five Love Languages"*, Tony Evans', *"Husband's Role in his Home*", Bishop TD Jakes', "*He-motions*", and Reverend Eric Lee's, "*Contempt at the Crib.*" I attended marriage enhancement classes, marriage conferences, marriage counseling and searched for everything and anything that I could find on having a successful marriage. After applying what I heard, I still didn't have a successful marriage. My wife still wasn't happy.

We learned each other's love language and began to apply the process and ideas from the "Five Love Languages" teaching. My wife was happy, and things looked great. However, this was short lived. She started complaining again and became very unhappy. In 2006, I was laid off from Grady Hospital, and my wife took my name off all our joint bank accounts and credit cards. She also didn't allow me to use any of the three cars that we had. She began to spread many lies about me including, that she was afraid for her safety. She had the Chairman of the Deacon Board of our church to come the house to protect her from me. This, my friends, was the "straw that broke the camel's back". As result, I became very frustrated and extremely hurt by this. I sought the Lord about why I was failing again, when I was trying to do the right things.

One of the answers I received was that some men are treated like "dogs" and some "dogs" are treated like men (kings). Most men who "dog out" their women would be worshipped and adored by that woman, but a man who worships a woman, that woman would "dog him out". I was told by someone that some women love "thugs" because it gives them excitement. "Nice" guys are too boring, and they want someone to dominate them (take charge).

Those answers didn't satisfy me, so I went to the one who invented marriage, God. I realized that if you want to know how a product should work, you must refer to the manufacturer's manual. So, I did. The information I received from God, the manufacturer, was so good that I felt the need to share it with everyone who wanted a successful marriage as much as I do.

One of the things that I learned was that happiness is based on things that happen. It is impossible to make someone happy, because that individual must *decide* to be happy. A person can have everything in the world and still be unhappy. One of the mistakes that I made in both of my marriages was, thinking it was my responsibility to make my spouses happy. I sought to please them rather than lead them. The Lord told me that even though He is a good God, He does not give us everything we want. The head of the house must take the position as the leader. As a leader, he must walk in purpose and leave a legacy for his family. The man must lead his family into their destiny. The word husband means "caretaker who protects, provides and takes care of his wife".

After my second marriage failed, I was at risk of my children not taking any advice from me about marriage going forward. I am sharing my own failures to let my readers know that they are not alone in their search for answers. Let me say it again, my experiences serve a greater purpose than just the discomfort I went through. What I learned from these experiences is being used to edify, educate and empower couples to conquer the issues in their marriage. The Lord revealed to me that marriage is a journey, and everyone has baggage they carry while on the journey. The challenge is how to handle the baggage.

I was blessed by my church, Light of the World Christian Tabernacle, who offered divorce care classes to those who were recently divorced. These sessions helped me to properly grieve the loss of my spouses, the losses of in-laws, the loss of homes, the loss of cars, and the loss of friends.

Just when I was convinced that marriage was not for me, everything changed. While visiting my Mom and Dad in the Bahamas, out of nowhere, I had a vision about a young lady with whom I was doing ministry with. The vision was of Pastor Ann and I going door-to-door, hand-in-hand, witnessing. After much disputing and wondering whether the vision I had was the result of me eating too much pork the night before, I returned to Atlanta and didn't say a word to anyone. Ann Avery was a Pastor at Light of the World where I attended church. She was a serious minister of the gospel. She was a kind hearted, loving and no-nonsense beautiful lady. We started to date in June.

In July, during Holy Convocation, Bishop John Pace of Florida (who didn't know that we were dating) told Pastor Ann to tell me that the Lord showed him that I was going to marry a preacher. As God would have it, her middle name is the same as my mother's first name, Pearl. A year later we were married, and we have been working together in ministry ever since. Since then, we have been installed as the Outreach Pastors for Light of the World. Indeed, my vision was real because we now work together in ministry providing training to churches' ministerial staff in the areas of outreach and evangelism. We also host a blog talk radio show that airs every Saturday night at 8 pm and we have our ministry website at http://www.butterfieldsministriesworldwide.com

We have faced challenges in our marriage, and have had to make changes in our habits, beliefs, and the effects of our family traits and unresolved issues. We are learning from these challenges and the changes are bringing us closer. Survival of conflict brings strength to relationships. We are working the principles of this book and it is working great for us.

I wrote this chapter to let you know that God has a plan for our lives. Where we were born, the family that we were born in, and the trauma that will impact our life, is to help us to produce or birth a solution for our trauma. My first and second wives caused me to seek the solution to divorce and separation. I wouldn't have ever wanted to know what it takes to have the marriage that God wanted us to have, if it was not for my experiences with my first and second wives. My third and present wife provided the confirmation of what God had revealed to me is the solution to separation and divorce. This marriage is allowing us to experience the marriage that God always wanted us to have. It is so good to love someone and great to have them really love you back!

I realized that I am chosen by God, and because the steps of a good man are ordered by the Lord, this life was chosen for me by God. God who knew that I would have two failed marriages and chose me before the world began. Therefore, I lived to talk about it to encourage and inspire you that you can make it too. It is also the inspiration of my music video on youtube.com called "Here I am". Feel free to take a look at what God gave to me at: https://www.youtube.com/watch?v=NPpDMHb6hfA

Thank you for your purchase, and my prayer is that you will receive the marriage that God has for you too!

Stephen A. Butterfield, Sr.

Part 1
Marriage

Chapter 1
Marriage: The Definition

Genesis 2:24 *"Therefore shall a man leave his father and his mother and shall cleave unto his wife and they shall be one flesh"*

Marriage involves meeting the needs of each spouse, with the knowledge and understanding of those needs, and using wisdom in meeting those needs. Marriage is the union of a man and a woman.

I believe that there are eight "C"s which must be followed and implemented in Marriage. They are as follows: Communication, Collaboration, Cohabitation, Consummation, Commitment, Consideration, Consistency and Compromise.

- **Communication** is a man and a woman speaking and listening with understanding.
- **Collaboration** is a man and a woman working together with clear communication.
- **Co-habitation** is a man and a woman living together with clear communication.
- **Consummation** is a man and a woman being intimate together with clear communication.
- **Commitment** is a man and a woman deciding to be together, "until death do they part", with clear communication.
- **Consideration** is a man and a woman being thoughtful and sensitive toward each other with clear communication.
- **Consistency** is a man and a woman being consistent in developing trust together with clear communication.
- **Compromise** is a man and a woman submitting to each other with clear communication.

Stephen A. Butterfield, Sr.

Discussion

Which "C" do you have under control?
Which "C" do you need help with?

Marriage the Journey

Stephen A. Butterfield, Sr.

Marriage: Ordained by God

"And the LORD *God said, it is not good that the man should be alone; I will make him a help meet for him. And the LORD God caused a <u>deep</u> sleep to fall upon <u>Adam</u>, and he slept: and he took one of his ribs, and closed up the <u>flesh</u> instead thereof. And the rib, which the LORD God had taken from man, made he a woman, and brought her unto the man. And <u>Adam</u> said, This is now bone of my bones, and <u>flesh</u> of my <u>flesh</u>: she shall be called Woman, because she was taken out of Man."* - Genesis 2:18, 21-23

The first marriage was officiated by God in the garden of Eden with Adam and Eve as the bride and the groom. Marriage was instituted by God to replenish the earth by producing fruits after its kind, to have dominion over the earth, and everything in and on the earth. Adam confirmed that they were one when he said to Eve, *"You are bones of my bones, and flesh of my flesh and you shall be called woman"*.

Marriage: Symbol of the Kingdom of God

"And I John saw the holy city, New Jerusalem, coming down from God out of heaven, prepared as a bride adorned for her husband." –Revelation 21:2

"Husbands love your wives even as Christ loves the church and gave himself for it." - Ephesians 5:25

Marriage is a symbol of the Kingdom of God. The Kingdom of God is about God's relationship with man, and marriage is a relationship between a husband and wife. God specializes in relationships. He came down in the cool of the day just to commune with, and have a relationship, with Adam. When people are born again, they become children of God and begin having a relationship with God. Marriage consists of two completely different people becoming one. God is the only one who can take two of anything and make it equal to one. God's nature is holy and even though man's nature is sinful, we can still become one with God (John 17:20). Jesus asks God to make him and the disciples one, as he and the father are one. The church is Jesus' bride, who is referred to as the body of Christ. Remember?

Divorce is more than just the destruction of marriage. It is the attack on the Kingdom of God. The institution of marriage has been under attack since its inception in the Garden of Eden. It was mentioned in Genesis, Chapter 3 with the fall of man. Being a Christian is not what a person does, it is who they are. Christianity is about having a relationship with God the Father. This relationship should inspire mankind to please God and yield not to temptation, just as a married couple resists the temptation to cheat on their spouse.

Men are typically built physically stronger than women and are typically not as sensitive or emotional as women are. It has been said that women typically are emotional, and men are physical and logical. Most women are verbal and express themselves that way. On the other hand, most men are non-verbal and internalize their feelings. They have a low threshold for pain unlike women, who bear the pain of childbirth and experience monthly cycles. It is said that men only use one side of their brain which deals with their ability to think logically, unlike women who use both sides of their brain.

Marriage is the bringing together of all these differences to work together in harmony, as a great and well-oiled machine. However, for it to work properly, it requires help from the one who created it, God; through the Holy Ghost.

Mankind is as different from God as men are different from women, even though the woman came from man and man was spoken out of God and made in His image and likeness. Sin made the difference. The only way this union and harmony is possible, in its fullness, is through the assistance of the Holy Ghost. The first thing the Holy Ghost will teach us is submission after we encounter Him.

Wait one-minute ladies! Submission is a word a lot of women have problems with because some men do not read the verse before it that states to "submit ye one to another". Hold up, men! God was the first to submit. Submission just means to give up one's will for another. God gave up His son to redeem us and, in that Jesus made the ultimate sacrifice to make the church his bride. (Ephesians 5).

Paul says in verse 33 that this is a great mystery, the husband and wife relationship, but he was speaking concerning Christ and the church. When we came to Jesus and received Him as our Savior, we had a lot of baggage. Once we get saved, we must get rid of our "sin" baggage. Those habits, beliefs, unresolved issues and family traits that are contrary to the will of God must be put out of our lives. We may have habits, traits and beliefs that are in accordance to God's will, so those traits, habits and beliefs we keep and allow the Holy Ghost to refine and perfect them.

Statistics say that more than 55% of marriages will end in divorce. The mindboggling thing about that statistic is that there is another 30% or more of couples who are just staying married for convenience, and the children. Some of them even sleep in separate bedrooms! Yes, there are marriages that are not working.

The statistics also show that the divorce rate in the church is higher, or just as high as that of secular marriages. Satan desires to destroy everything that God has established. He thinks that if he can get the family, then he can stop the church!

Stephen A. Butterfield, Sr.

Discussion

How is marriage the symbol of the Kingdom?

Marriage the Journey

JEWISH WEDDINGS

The Jewish wedding ceremonies are twofold. The betrothal occurs when the father of the groom chooses the bride for his son. Our

Father (God) chooses the church, which is the bride of Christ (we were chosen by God). The son then has to walk to the village and give a dowry (payment) to the father of the bride to claim the right to have her as his bride. Jesus came to earth and paid a dowry for us. After this, the bride begins preparing for the wedding day and the groom returns home to build a room on his father's house.

Jesus went back to the father and is preparing a place for His bride, the church. The church (bride) is now preparing for Jesus' (groom) return. The father of the groom (God) chooses the wedding day and the groom would only know the date when his father tells him. Jesus does not know the day of His return. On the day that the father chooses, the groom will go to the bride's father's house and return with the bride to his father's house where the ceremony would take place. Jesus is taking the church to the place that he has prepared for his bride, the church. The wedding ceremony is where the covenant is made and later consummated.

Marriage:
The Journey

Marriage is a peregrination, which means a long and meandering journey. Marriage is not a destination, but it is a journey. Statistics say, that if a small business doesn't fail within the first five years, then they will be successful. However, the same is not true for marriages, because there is no such thing as making it past five years and being set for life. The definition of the word journey is a passage. In other words, it means a travel through time in different conditions, atmospheres and seasons. The journey is what happens between the beginning and the end. It is from the time when "I do" is said until death.

Marriage is full of changes, different periods, or intervals, and with those changes comes different challenges. Yes, it's the experience of sharing everything with someone. Husbands and wives are expected to make life changing decisions with each other's best interest in mind, not just their own. They are expected to love one another and only that person for the rest of their lives. Yes, they should love unconditionally even when their libido is raging and when it has gone; when they have hair and when they don't; when the times are good and when they are bad; when she has menopause and he has a mid-life crisis; when there is only the two of them and when there are 10; when there is an empty nest and when they are starting careers; and when they are retiring or even changing careers.

In life, the only thing that is constant is change. Understanding these changes is complicated and understanding the changes that happen in marriages are even more complicated. Relationships and marriages are affected by the baggage each person brings into the relationship or marriage. The first stage or period of marriage is one of marital bliss, where many things are overlooked because of the excitement of being married. During this period a couple's tolerance level for one another's baggage is extremely high so that a lot of the things that they don't like to get overlooked and are accepted. The next stage is when reality kicks in and their differences are noticed and discussed. These are the challenges. This is the stage where the baggage is exposed, and couples start tripping

Stephen A. Butterfield, Sr.

and falling over their baggage. This book is to help you avoid tripping over your baggage.

Part 2
Preparation for the Journey

Chapter 2

Premarital Counseling

"For which of you intending to build a tower, sitteth not down first, and counteth the cost, whether he have sufficient to finish it" - Luke 14:28

Preparation is the key ingredient for success in everything in life. Athletes know that preparation is more important than the game itself. Coaches know that preparation starts before practice time. They research the team scheduled to be played by watching tapes, and even attending some of their opponents' games, looking for certain tendencies or traits. They may notice that their opponents run the full court press for the entire game, or only the second half. Coaches will conduct practices on how to break their opponents' press. Once the necessary preparation has been made, the only thing necessary during the game is to make adjustments in plays and personnel.

The same holds true in marriages. Once the necessary preparation is made in the beginning, the only thing needed throughout the marriage is adjustment, which is better known as compromise. Compromise is the attitude of whatever it takes to win. It does not matter who scores the most points, but that team wins the game. Basketball legend, Michael Jordan is the best player to ever play the game of basketball. Early in his career he would score 50 to 65 points, but his team would still lose the game. It was not until other players like Scottie Pippen, BJ Armstrong, and Horace Grant began to contribute to the game that the Chicago Bulls were able to create a basketball dynasty by winning several championships.

In marriage, the goal is to have a great marriage, not individual success because the marriage is a team. It doesn't matter who makes the most money. If the wife makes the most money, her position on the team does not change because the husband is still the head of the household and is responsible and liable for its success. If the wife is a better administrator than the husband, the team still wins when she takes care of writing out the bills and they get paid on time. If the husband is a better cook than the wife, and more domesticated, let everyone use their individual gifts and grace for the success of the marriage.

Marriage is not to be entered in unadvisedly, but discreetly and advisedly. Couples should not ever get married or think about getting married without receiving premarital counseling. Premarital counseling is equal to consulting with a travel agent before planning a trip. As the counselor, the travel agent will go over with their clients the information needed for the journey they are about to go on. They will tell them the type of weather to expect, and the type of transportation needed to get them from one place to the other. The counselor will tell them that there will be days when conflicts will come up and how to handle those conflicts and bad weather days. The counselor will teach them how to be intimate with their mate, by becoming so close to them that they can almost read their mind. They will teach them also how to compromise. Each person will express their individual expectations for this journey; yes, their expectation for their marriage. As the travel agent gives them the itinerary, the counselor will provide them with a layout of marriage. As with a natural journey, after returning from the travel agency with the itinerary in hand, a client will begin to take out all the stuff (clothing, shoes, hats, etc....), trying to decide what they will take on this journey. After receiving premarital counseling, a couple should be figuratively naked before each other and pull out all their baggage. When Eve was brought to Adam, she came naked. He saw exactly what he was getting: no wig, no dentures, no girdles, etc. Strip down to your birthday suit!

There must first be an agreement and a commitment from both parties that each one will do whatever it takes for the journey to be great. The husband-to-be should be the first to pull out all his stuff. Yes, he should make a list of all his likes, dislikes, turn-offs, turn-ons, good and bad habits, good and bad traits, good and bad beliefs, all the things he hates about himself, all the things he likes about himself, and everything else related. I have heard people say that in order to get your license to become a doctor, nurse, CPA, or dentist you must first pass a test. But in marriage, licenses are given first, then the test comes. This should not be the case. God intended for parents to act as the authorized trainers of their children for marriage. However, one of the biggest problems I see is that most parents do not do a good enough job of training their children to be good husbands and good wives. Most people are taught how to be independent men and women, but hardly ever are they taught how to be a husband or wife. Parents should be training and drilling their children during their formative years on what it takes to be a good husband or a good wife. Also, parents should teach them how to work well with others – especially their siblings. When this does not happen a struggle in a marriage occurs. Parents should not have to take all the blame because no one told them what they should be doing.

The following is what I believe should happen. Sons should be able to see their father submitting to the cares and concerns of his wife and family, while at the same time, submitting to God's word. Likewise, daughters should see their mother submitting to the father while she is submitting to God's word. If this happens, daughters would learn authority and how to submit to authority, and the sons will learn their responsibilities as servant leaders.

When daughters get married, the authority of covering is transferred to their husband which is why it is a tradition to ask, "Who gives this woman to be married?" before the groom takes his bride. The father then passes the authority in covering to the groom. When the vows are exchanged, the officiator says to the groom "*I now pronounce you man and wife. You may kiss your bride.*" It is at that time that the groom lifts the veil allowing him to be intimate with his bride. The husband now has the authority to go beyond the veil. When Jesus died for our sins, the veil in the temple was ripped open signifying that all believers can enter the holiest of holy and experience intimacy with God.

After identifying all the baggage by getting naked and exposing themselves, a revelation of their fiancé (fiancée) would come. They would gain knowledge of the traits, habits and beliefs of their spouse-to-be. Just as God loves his children after knowing everything about them, engaged couples must love their intended. This information is not to be used against their intended but should be used to learn about them with the hopes of understanding them better. They will see why they do what they do. This is the time when they should decide if they still want to marry this person. Each person must decide which beliefs, habits, unresolved issues and family traits need to be modified and modify them. For example, should the toilet paper roll up or down, or should the toothpaste be squeezed from the bottom, middle, or the top.

The baggage that must be understood and handled correctly are those that deal with relationship and love. Marriage is a journey; therefore, baggage must be included. The main problem in most marriages is the handling of the baggage appropriately. Again, a natural journey is where individuals would go to a travel agent, plan their journey and then the travel agent would then give them an itinerary. But this does not happen in most marriages, and as a result marriages fail. Every baggage that you have may not be good to take with you on a certain journey. On a journey to Alaska, no one would take swimming trunks or bathing suits with them. The same precautions must be made when considering marriage. As was previously mentioned in the earlier chapter, baggage is the thing that affects an individual's mindset. It is their beliefs, habits, unresolved issues and family traits. These are carried with them everywhere they go and affect their perception of everything. Perception dictates how individuals respond to everything. Perception is more real than reality. The real issue with these four aspects of baggage is that they make an individual who they are. People respond to certain situations without thinking because of their beliefs, family traits, unresolved issues and habits.

Discussion

*Did you have premarital counseling?
What was the most important thing that you
learned in your premarital counseling?*

Marriage the Journey

Part 3
Naked
&
Exposed
"The Baggage"

Stephen A. Butterfield, Sr.

Chapter 3
Baggage: Who Are You, Really?

"And Adam said: This is now bone of my bones and flesh; She shall be called Woman, because she was taken out of man. And they were both naked the man and his wife and were not ashamed."- Genesis 2:23 and 25

Our baggage, as it relates to relationships, is typically thoughts that individuals bring from past relationships into their new relationship. I believe that unresolved issues from the past was only one fourth of what God has given me about baggage. When I say baggage, I am referring to those idiosyncrasies that make us different from everyone else. When I say baggage, I am referring to the things people do without thinking or how it may affect others, because they have always done things the way they have. It has now become a law that they live by and they are convinced that it must be right, because it is how they have always done things.

Now, all baggage is not bad. Baggage is the things that people are born with, trained in, and "learned" through experiences. One must be very careful about using unresolved issues as a barometer for their current decisions because they can distort their ability to make a sound decision. The essence of baggage is a soul issue. Baggage attaches to a person's will, their emotions and their thoughts, according to Genesis 2:7-8, that says, *"And the* LORD *God formed man of the dust of the ground, and breathed into his nostrils the breath of life; and man became a living soul."* The breath of God made man God's will, God's feelings and God's thinking. Genesis 2:16-17 says, *"And the LORD God commanded the man, saying, 'Of every tree of the garden thou mayest freely eat: But of the tree of the knowledge of good and evil, thou shalt not eat of it: for in the day that thou eatest thereof thou shalt surely die."*

The knowledge of good and evil destroyed and corrupted the soul of man. Man was no longer a living soul. Man's perception changed immediately. How he looked at things changed. How he felt about things changed. How he thought about things changed. His will, emotions and thoughts became separated from God, which is death. Being naked was natural, but after sin, Adam saw nakedness and then he felt ashamed and embarrassed. Now man's thought was to cover up and hide. But, to get the soul right again, we need the redemption that is in the finished work of Jesus Christ. King David said that, "He restoreth my soul and leadeth me in the path of righteousness for His name sake".

If marriage is a journey, then there must be traveling, and if there is traveling, there must be baggage. Have you ever gone to the airport in preparation to travel and found out that your luggage was too heavy, and to continue your journey you had to pay extra for your baggage? The same is true in marriage; having too much baggage can cost a couple. Unnecessary baggage will also cost a couple.

I believe there are four (4) things that affect how we see, feel, think and act. The four things are: your *beliefs, habits, unresolved issues, and family traits.* Every experience in our lives shapes and forms our perspective. Our perspectives are formed by things that are deposited in each person which adds to their beliefs, habits or family traits. Each has its purpose. After Adam sinned, he became self-centered instead of God-centered because of the knowledge of good and evil.

Stephen A. Butterfield, Sr.

Discussion

*Did you really expose yourself to each other?
Is there anything that your spouse does not know
about you?*

Chapter 4
Family Traits: Traditions

Family Traits – These are some of the things that families live by and teach their offspring as rules to live by. Families are known for how they carry themselves whether good or bad. Some call family traits generational curses, but not all family traits are bad. I am sure you have seen families where mostly everyone is an educator, teacher, accountant, lawyer, etc. It is that behavior that is identified with that family.

Some people call them personality traits. I strongly suggest that during the dating period, after you both decide that the relationship has a long-term possibility, you attend several family gathering with your fiancé (fiancée). You will see how they interact with their family members. I believe that a son who is kind to his mother has a great potential to be a great and caring husband. Vice-versa, a daughter who is kind to her father has a great potential to be a great wife. This is my take and you can call it Butterfield 101. Also, please disclose family medical history. I recommend couples using the genogram. This standardized genogram format is common now for tracking family history and relationships (McGoldrick, Gerson & Petry, 2008).

In the Bible, Jacob, whose name means under handed, being a trickster, crook, or "slickster" was a family trait. His uncle, Laban, tricked him into marrying Leah in Genesis 30. His mother, Laban's niece, Rachel, helped Jacob trick his father into believing he was Esau in Genesis 27. It was a family trait. Remember David? He was a womanizer. He took a man's wife, Bathsheba, and then set him up to be killed. David's son, Amnon, loved his sister and raped her (2 Samuel 13). And please don't forget his son Solomon who had 700 wives and 300 concubines.

Abram and Isaac, father and son told the same lie under the same circumstances, about their wives being their sisters to save their own lives. They both had some beautiful wives and had good taste in women.

Couples need to understand each other's family in order to understand what each person is capable of *before* you get married. What is their family medical history, financial history, education and emotional history?

In the Bahamas, where I was born and raised, when a young man is interested in dating a young lady, he had to ask the father for permission to date her. The first question the father would ask the young man was, **"WHO'S YA PEOPLE?"** The answer to this question would let the father know what the young man's potential and capabilities were. Every family had a reputation and were judged based on their family's reputation.

My maternal grandfather's family traits were musicians and educators. While my maternal grandmother's family traits were transparent. Meaning, if they thought of you a certain way you would hear it from them face to face, and never behind your back without animosity. My paternal grandparents were unknown to me.

The following is a list of other family traits. See if yours is listed. Loudness or Quiet; Discreet or Vulgar; Alcoholics or Sober; Lazy or Workaholic; Educated or Illiterate.

Marriage the Journey

Discussion

*Do you know your spouse's family traits?
Would it hurt or help your marriage?*

Stephen A. Butterfield, Sr.

Chapter 5
Love Expressions

Love is very important in marriage. We must identify what love looks like to each person. Just like the spoken language, we all have different ways that we identify love. The reason this chapter is place in the section called family traits is because we identify love most of the time based on how our family demonstrated love to us while growing up. Therefore, each spouse may demonstrate or receive love differently. So, it is important that they know how each other look at love. If one of the spouses is not aware of the other spouse's love expression, then that spouse will not feel loved by their spouse. For example, if the wife's love expression is quality time and the husband's is physical touch. The husband will show is affection by caressing her, thinking that his spouse would know by this act that he loves her. But she feels unloved because she feels that all he wants is sex, and not to just spend time with her. The Five Love Languages cover some of these, as far as, understanding how individuals interpret what love means to them.

A person's love expression is based primarily on how they were shown love in their early years. For example, some parents are very affectionate, some just give their children the things they need, some spend quality time with them, some always affirm their children, and some always give them gifts. When your fiancé (fiancée) does what your parents did, you will receive it as an act of love. Individuals must identify their own love expression, and the love expression of their fiancé (fiancée) and then show them love in their love language. Just like when a family is born in Germany, the children and parents speak German. If they move to the United States, they must learn to speak English. The same principle applies when entering a marriage – each intended must learn a new language. Everyone can learn a new way to express love.

"The Five Love Languages" by Gary Chapman is a really great book that explains them. I will share briefly each of the five love languages and how being aware of them can save marriages. Mr. Chapman described the Five Love Languages as keeping your love tank filled by your spouse. The Five Love Languages are as follows:

1. Physical Touch
2. Words of Affirmation
3. Quality Time
4. Acts of Service
5. Receiving Gifts

Physical Touch – *Love touches may be explicit and demand your full attention, such as foreplay culminating in intercourse and it can be implicit requiring moments such and rubbing bodies in passing* (Chapman, 1984). Other examples are, when your family shows you love with hugs and kisses, when holding hands or when rubbing your shoulders or back. So, when your spouse gives you hugs and kisses, this satisfies your LOVE JONES.

Words of Affirmation – *Verbal compliments and words of appreciation are great communicators of love. When we receive affirming words, we are far more likely to be motivated to reciprocate.* (Chapman, 1984) This is when your family shows you love by telling you that you are beautiful and saying "good job" when you do anything or when your spouse compliments you and tells you that he/she loves you.

Quality Time – This is when you receive special attention by your loved one. *This person needs their spouse to maintain eye contact when they are speaking privately to their spouse; not to listen while doing something else; listen with feelings; observe their body language; and refuse to interrupt.* (Chapman, 1984). This is when your family shows you love by spending time together. When your spouse spends time with you and gives you their undivided attention, this demonstrates love to you.

Acts of Service – *Ask your spouse to make a list of ten things they would like for you to do during the next month. Then ask them to prioritize and use this list to plan your strategy for a month of love* (Chapman, 1984). This is when your family shows love by making sure that you have everything that you need. When your spouse, if you are a male, washes the dishes, vacuums the carpet, folds the clothes, etc. This will satisfy your LOVE JONES.

Receiving Gifts – *Gifts need not be expensive, nor must they be weekly because with some people the gift worth has nothing to do with monetary value and everything to do with love* (Chapman, 1984). This is when your family shows you love by buying you gifts on every occasion, birthdays, holidays, etc... When your spouse buys you gifts on every occasion and just because they
love you, this also satisfies your LOVE JONES.

Marriage the Journey

Discussion

Do you know your spouse's love language? How would you relate to your spouse's love language?

Stephen A. Butterfield, Sr.

What is Love?

Jesus said unto him, thou shalt love the Lord thy God with all thy heart, and with all thy soul, and with all thy mind. – Matthew 22:37-38

In the 1970's Flip Wilson said that *"love is a feeling that you feel when you are about to feel a feeling that you never felt before."* It sounds good, but love should not be based on feelings, because feelings change by the seconds. Love is a ***committed*** decision. However, there is a brain activity that occurs when you fall in love, which is the "butterfly in your stomach" feeling. This is called ***Phenethylamine (PEA).*** This feeling only lasts a maximum of 2 years. After this period, both parties decide to be committed to each other.

God expects each spouse to love each other, even with their baggage. God knows all about us and He still loves us! He wants us to love Him with everything that we have. Husbands and wives should love with their SOUL, their WILL, their MIND and their EMOTIONS. Yes, their SOUL; I must say "I do" for better or worse, for richer or poorer, in sickness or in health, until death do, we part. Familial love, love for your family, will not make it; Eros love, love for your lover will not make it; ONLY AGAPE will do -- Yes, God's love. After exposing ourselves and being completely NAKED, it's going to take the unconditional love of God to love your spouse. I encourage you to purchase a best seller book called, "A Word On Love" by Dr. Ruth W. Smith in order to get more insight on the Agape love. We must first acknowledge our baggage, and yes get NAKED!

Stephen A. Butterfield, Sr.

Discussion

Do you love your spouse because of, or in spite of?

Sex Talk

"Marriage is honorable in all, and the bed undefiled: but whoremongers and adulterers God will judge." - Hebrews 13:4

Sex deals with one of the C's in a successful marriage which is **Consummation**. Consummation is a vital part of marriage. Sex is so important that even after the wedding ceremony, if there is no consummation, the marriage can be voided by law (Annulment). It is as if the wedding never took place if there was no consummation. Sex is more than a physical act; it is a spiritual act. Two souls become one through consummation. The saying, "love making" for sex indicates that sex is a way to create and express love. Sex is so important, that God does not want you to fast unless it is agreed upon by a couple.

"Do not deprive one another, except perhaps by agreement for a limited time, that you may devote

yourselves to prayer; but then come together again, so that Satan may not tempt you because of your lack of self-control." - 1 Corinthians 7:5

    The importance of sex in marriage supports the need for a discussion. Sexual preferences must be discussed before a couple gets married. Sex may end in the bed, but it begins when you wake up in the morning. How do you express love when you first open your eyes in the morning? Then, how do you express love during the day and when you reunite for dinner? Sex becomes the apex of the expression of love.

    Sex is more enjoyable when there is passion. Passion is high when each person is pleased with their spouse's behavior towards them. The smaller the conflict or contention, the greater the passion. The greater the conflict and contention, the smaller the passion. So, to increase the passion in the bedroom is to reduce the conflict and contention. Seek peace in the home, and you will get a "piece" in the bed (sex).

Marriage the Journey

Below are some suggested questions that couples should ask about sex before they get married.

Stephen A. Butterfield, Sr.

Discussion

What is your sexual preference?
Is oral sex agreeable with you?
Are you comfortable with your body?
How many times a week, a day, a month would you like to have sex?
Do you like foreplay?

Chapter 6
Beliefs:
Firmly Held Convictions

Beliefs are the core values that were taught throughout each person's life. To complicate things even more, these values sometimes change based on certain events that happen in their lives such as, an unsaved person getting saved, or a person experiencing tragedy or illness.

Religious beliefs are a whole other issue by themselves: Baptists, Methodists, Catholics, Jewish, Atheists, Pentecostal Holiness, etc.....

Solomon was the wisest man that ever lived, other than Jesus, but he became a fool when he served the gods of the strange women he married. They were strange women because they served other gods than the God almighty.

2 Corinthians 6:14 says, *"Be ye not unequally yoked together with unbelievers."* Christians must be careful not to become entangled with Christians who have different beliefs than they do. For example, a female who is called of God and knows she is, may meet a Christian male who believes that females should keep silent in the church. 1 Corinthians 14:34 says, *"Let your women keep silent in the church."* If those two individuals decide to get married, she, being the submissive faithful obedient wife, would have to choose whether to obey the call of God on her life or the demands of her husband. Some people don't believe that women should be in leadership in the church, though I don't know where they get that idea from. Deborah was a judge over the children of Israel, and a female leader chosen by God. God is the same yesterday, today and forever according to Judges 4:4.

The following are a few scenarios to illustrate this point:

Thou shall not steal. One individual may believe they should not steal, and their spouse may believe they can if they do not get caught. These spouses will soon find themselves at odds. One spouse will find themselves compromising their values. Sooner or later they will begin stealing from each other. This will eventually birth mistrust, thus the deterioration of the relationship and marriage. Even if they are not stealing from each other, suspicion is going to be there if anything comes up missing. Again, trust is destroyed.

Thou shall not bear false witness. One individual may believe that telling any lie is wrong, but the other may believe they can tell little "white ones" when necessary. News flash! There is no such thing as a white or a little lie. Remember, sin came into the world by the lie Satan told Eve in Genesis 3 that says, *"If you eat of the tree of the knowledge of good and evil you will not surely die."* Lies will also destroy the trust an individual has in their mate and cause them to not know when they are telling the truth.

I stated earlier in my introduction about my father having married so many times. I learned that one of his beliefs was that "he should not have sex with any woman who he was not married to." So, when he met someone who he wanted to have sex with, he would divorce the one he was with, and marry the new one. He did this over eight times in his life span. I also believe that you should not have sex with someone who you are not married to, but I also believe that you should be married for life and not change spouses like you change your clothes.

General beliefs are traditions passed down from generation to generation and become a way of life. There are some people, women and men who believe that it is okay for men to have many sexual partners, but women should not. They live their lives with this belief and pass it on to their children. A young girl may tell her mother about her boyfriend cheating her, and the mother, who believes that it's okay for men to have multiple sexual partners would say to her, "Oh, girl, he is just being a man." This is a

Marriage the Journey

belief that you shouldn't have. If you have it, you need to get rid of it, whether you are a man or a woman.

Here are few examples of such general beliefs:

1. Be independent or no man is an island.
2. One spouse believes men should be able to do housework, and the other believes that men should not do housework. So, if the male spouse believes that he should not do any housework and the wife believes that he should, there will be contempt at the crib. (Pastor Eric Lee)
3. If one spouse believes in dressing modest or in dressing vulgar.
4. Be courteous or be mean spirited.
5. Do unto others as they do to you or do unto others as you would have them do unto you.
6. The man should handle all financial issues or have separate bills.
7. Sleep with married people or never consider being with married people.
8. Spear the rod, spoil the child or use time-outs, not the rod.

9. Husband is the head of the household, or whoever has the most income is head of the household.
10. A good name is better than gold or don't care about how people see you.
11. Husbands who don't have their own house and doesn't pay all the household bills is not the head of his house.
12. It is bad luck to have dirty clothes and a dirty house to bring in the New Year.
13. It is good luck to eat black eyed peas on New Years' Day.
14. Be loyal or be with whoever pleases you at the time.

Just to name a few.

Discussion

*Which of your spouse's beliefs surprises you?
Explain your different beliefs.
Do they need professional help with it?*

Chapter 7
Habits

Habits are things that an individual has been doing most or all their lives. Therefore, they are things which people do without even thinking. They are learned behaviors that are practiced over time. Most of the time it will take a major event in their lives to change them. Every habit must be discussed: spending, working, drinking, smoking, grooming, living, and any other habit you can think of.

There is a story of a mother who always cut her ham in half before she placed in the oven. One day someone asked her why; she didn't know it was because it was what she saw her mother do. She became curious and asked her mother, who then told her that it was what her grandmother did it back in the day because their oven was too small to cook the whole ham!

This is just an example of how habits form and become a part of who we are.

The following are a few examples:
1. Squeezing the toothpaste from the bottom, or middle of the tube
2. Eating at a special time of the day, i.e. must eat at 6 pm
3. Do not wear shoes in the house, must take shoes off at the front door
4. Non-smoker or chain smoker
5. Alcohol drinker or drug addict
6. Hang clothes behind or on doors
7. Neatness or slob
8. Orderly or clustered
9. Promiscuous or Monogamous
10. Night owl, stays up late at night

Discussion

*Which of your spouse's habits surprise you?
Do they need professional help with it?*

Chapter 8
Unresolved Issues

Unresolved issues are components of who we really are based on a trauma or loss that happened in our past, which we have not properly grieved for. Our thinking, feelings and behavior can be influenced by unresolved issues. Unresolved issues can result in mental illness such as anxiety, middle child syndrome, Napoleonic complex, bipolar disorder, and much more. Because individuals dealing with unresolved issues are not easily identified, the recommendation is that anyone who has ever had a relationship which ended involuntarily needs a check-up. Yes, counseling.

While taking and teaching the class on divorce care for people going through a divorce or separation, I have learned that when individuals separate from their lovers it is not just simply a separation, but a tear. Therefore, they are not whole, and mending takes time to heal. A big problem happens when people do not get healed before they begin another relationship: hurting people, hurt people. Consciously they may feel well and healed, but subconsciously they may not be.

Insecurity is a very dangerous symptom of an unresolved issue in marriage and relationship. Insecurities can stem from how an individual may view themselves, their opinion of themselves or from traumatic experiences throughout their lifetime. Insecurities hinder an individual's ability to trust. Trust is vital to a healthy relationship and marriage. Insecurities also produce anxiety. An individual who witnessed infidelity in their parents, siblings, neighborhood and their past relationships may find it had to trust their mate based on what they have seen down through the years. These individuals may even develop their own definition to cheating. Every action looks like cheating in their eyes. Paranoia will take place. If their spouse compliments a husband and wife (male and female), they would say that the compliment to the female was flirting, therefore, cheating. The sad thing about this situation is, the individual may never recognize that they are insecure and that they need to resolve the issue that caused them to become insecure. This individual can have access and the passwords of the spouse's cell phone and computer, and they will still believe that their spouse is cheating on them. Their spouse can be with them 90% of the time, and the other 10% of the time they communicate where they are before they depart from each other; and they would still think that they spouse is cheating on them.

Insecurities also come from when a woman doesn't think that she is beautiful or have a shapely body. When a beautiful lady comes around their spouse, before he can even look the beautiful lady's way, the insecure wife would accuse him of disrespecting her. If an incident looks similar or sounds like the cheating ex-lover, it will be looked at by the insecure spouse as cheating. Insecurity causes anxiety and anxiety causes contention. King Solomon, a very wise man, said that it was better to be on a rooftop, than in a large room with a contentious woman.

Some individuals have lost their heart to their ex-husband, ex-lover and never get it back. Some have their hearts back, but it is still broken. It is impossible to love without a heart, and it is impossible to love with a broken heart. There must be a way to retrieve those lost hearts and mend those broken hearts.

Rev. Al Green asked a question back in the 70's "How do you mend a broken heart? How do you stop the rain from falling down?" It seems impossible at the time but with therapy and the help of God, you can be whole again.

If you ended a relationship with a broken heart, did your heart ever get mended? Did you get your heart back? Does your "ex" still have your heart? Some people refuse, or are unable, to love again. No matter how many relationships they get involved in, they never love again. Many people stop loving. Many lives end in suicide and some just go through life never living. They find themselves stuck and cannot move on. Some people get involved in other relationships trying to get their hearts back. These people are very suspicious, insecure and will see deception in everything. These people many times don't know or aren't aware that they are stuck. Everyone needs to examine their ability to love before entering a relationship, especially a marriage. Individuals should do themselves, and the poor souls they are about to marry, a favor and stay single until they are able to have a healthy relationship. It is a tough thing to do and it will take God and professional help to move on.

Unresolved issues can influence the person's beliefs and habits. Insecurity can cause a person to believe that all men cheat; and they will treat all men they meet as cheaters.

Stephen A. Butterfield, Sr.

Discussion

*Which of your spouse's unresolved issues surprises you?
Do they need professional help with it?*

Marriage the Journey

Part 4
Children

Stephen A. Butterfield, Sr.

Chapter 9

Children

"Train up a child in the way he should go: and when he is old, he will not depart from it." - Proverbs 22:6

Instill in your children positive family traits, habits, and beliefs. Avoid as much as possible damaging your children's spirit with *your* drama. A parent's habits, family traits and beliefs *can* create unresolved issues for their children and will impact who they become.

Parenting styles are vital when raising children. Authoritarian, permissive, and uninvolved parents are qualities that are listed in the "Development Across the Life Span" as behaviors that can be detrimental to child development. Girls raised by **authoritarian parents** tend to be especially dependent on their parents and boys tend to become hostile and or aggressive. Children raised by **permissive parents** tend to be moody and display a lack of social skills and self-control. Children raised by **authoritative parents** tend to be friendly with peers, self-assertive and cooperative, and typically are successful and likable. **Uninvolved parents** tend to have children who become indifferent to their surroundings (Feldman, R. 2011).

Children bring another set of challenges to an already complicated situation in marriage. The information in this chapter is given to bring about an awareness of some things to think about as it relates to the subject of children. We must teach our children to be polite, courteous, kind, trustworthy, considerate, loyal, dependable, honest, and understanding. Please know that an individual's baggage (habits, family traits, beliefs and unresolved issues) will determine their pro-action, action and reaction.

Childbirth

A woman will experience physical and emotional changes in her body that will cause her eating and sleeping habits to change. The man must compensate by being supportive, but before this, the couple should discuss a few important questions. For example:

Should we plan our pregnancies?
How many children would we like to have?
When should we have children?

Childcare

How children will be cared for is also critical in a relationship and marriage. Other questions that need to be considered are:

Should the mother quit working to take care of the children?
Should only individuals in the family be allowed to babysit the children?
How do/should we toilet train the children?
Should we capture every first thing the children do?
How should we discipline the children?

Child Schooling

A vital part of children rearing involves children attending school. So, there are many questions that must be addressed:

At what age should the children begin school?

Should they be homeschooled?
Should they attend private or public school?
Should they be involved with extra-curricular activities (sports, band, etc.)?
Should they go to college?
Should they enlist in the military service?

Children in a Blended Family

Couples that bring children to the marriage face challenges as well. The questions that need to be asked are:

How can we help our children live together as brothers and sisters?
How do we raise our non-biological children?

One other significant point to consider is, please don't hinder your children in any way from having a relationship with their biological parent AND their step-parent.

Stephen A. Butterfield, Sr.

Part 5
Finances

Chapter 10
Finances

According to studies, finance is one the major causes of divorce and destruction of marriage. In a world where we must take care of ourselves, married couples sometimes forget that they are committed to have a new life with another individual. Couples fight about money twice as much as they fight about sex, according to a "Money Magazine" survey.

I must share some great financial advice that I received from a financial advisor named, Carol Pierre. First, bring your household expenses current. Then, set up an initial emergency fund of $1,000. Next, pay off your debt and buy term life insurance to cover ten years of your annual household income, amount of your mortgage, education or college costs for your children or yourself. Lastly, fully fund your emergency fund with three to six months of your total monthly household expenses.

Credit Scores

A good credit score is important for everyone to have. Loans are a necessary part of life for most of us. Building a solid credit history and maintaining a high credit score can have a dramatic impact on your quality of life now and in the future when you may be considering applying for a loan.

Couples should be educated about the importance of a good credit score. They need to learn how to obtain a good credit score and how to maintain it.

Spending Habits

Good spending habits are very important to couples. What everyone *doesn't* know is that good spending habits are just as important to your financial success as saving money or getting rid of your debt. Smart spending habits keep you from paying too much for an item.

Couples must consider their current spending habits and then discuss the adjustments that are needed to be financially stable.

https://www.everydollar.com/blog/create-better-spending-habits

Saving Habits

Now, I know this all sounds good in theory. I know only too well how difficult it is to save in your early working years when you are paying a mortgage, sending children to school and so on but, with a little discipline it can be done. The old adage of "pay yourself first" has never been more important. Make a commitment to save a set amount from your income (say 10%) and budget your expenses with the remaining 90%. It's an unfortunate situation when only 1 in 5 people seek financial advice. That's a far greater percentage in comparison to those who are in retirement, and the number of younger people who are doing so, is far less than 1 in 5.

Investing Habits

Investing habits are also very important for marriage relationship success. Investing mitigates against long-term illness, unemployment, and uncertainty of the future.

I suggest the following five habits of investing to couples which are: setting a goal, create a plan, save regularly, live on less, and stay in the game (Richard Buck, 2014).

Discussion

What is your spending habit?
What is your saving habit?
Do you know each other's credit score?
Do you need professional help?

Stephen A. Butterfield, Sr.

Part 6
Mid-Life Crisis & Menopause

Chapter 11
Mid-Life Crisis & Menopause

Mid-life crises occur when men begin to feel a sense of loss due to age and make lifestyle changes to compensate for it. They begin to lose their hair, energy, sex drive, mobility and physique. To compensate, they may do some unusual things like buy a motor cycle or a sports car, cut their hair differently, or change their dress style. That out-going, fun-loving guy may become a homebody, or the homebody may become an out-going, fun-loving guy. Anyway, the man that a woman may have come to know, may become someone else and she must now get to know this new guy.

Menopause is when a woman experiences the physical changes of life that may bring on many changes that they don't always understand themselves. Consequently, they too, begin to make changes to compensate. They may sometimes feel unattractive, and like men, they begin to lose their hair, energy, mobility and figure. Some women's sex drive increases with age. Just like men, their personalities may change and cause everyone in the house to have to get to know her all over again.

Marriage the Journey

Part 7
Baggage Handler

Stephen A. Butterfield, Sr.

Chapter 12
Identify the Baggage

Baggage is not necessarily bad, but it affects an individual's thoughts and actions. It is made up of those things that a person has been doing the same way most or all their lives. Baggage are those things that dictate how an individual think and responds to everything. Baggage is what makes up an individual—his or her morals, behavior and mindset, which are formed through their family traits, beliefs, unresolved issues and habits. How should individuals handle their baggage? It takes a lot of work because it speaks about changing the things they do, and the habits they have developed through the years.

I believe that the way to handle the baggage in your marriage is to become intimate with your spouse.

Intimacy

"Therefore, shall a man leave his father and his mother, and shall cleave unto his wife: and they shall be one flesh." – Genesis 2:24

I believe that INTIMACY is the answer to handling each spouse's baggage. As you LEAVE your father and mother (the family traits, habits, beliefs and unresolved issues) and CLEAVE: to join or cling (encounter, submission, and transformation) you become ONE (shall be one flesh).

"Real intimacy makes us feel alive like we've been found, as if someone finally took the time to peer

into the depths of our soul and really see us there. Until then, until we experience true intimacy, we will feel passed over and ignored, like someone is looking right through us. Sadly, we can miss out on intimacy that can make us and another person feel known, when we predetermine what we think we should see when we examine their life, heart, personality and soul. When this happens, we will try to mold and make them into who we believe they should be, and love and intimacy are destroyed." (Schutte, 2009).

Marriage the Journey

ENCOUNTER

SUBMISSION

TRANSFORMATION

ONENESS

Stephen A. Butterfield, Sr.

Discussion

*How do you show each other real intimacy?
Which of the four components of intimacy are you in?*

Chapter 13
Step 1: Encounter

"In the year that King Uzziah died, I saw the Lord, high and exalted, seated on a throne; and the train of his robe filled the temple" - Isaiah 6:1

The first step in intimacy is encounter. Encounter is to have a one-on-one in-depth experience with someone. Isaiah served in the temple for years, but never met the one that he was serving. Just like Paul/Saul who was employed by the church to execute the law of God but didn't meet God until the road to Damascus. Encounter is each person getting naked and exposed. You must show your fiancé (fiancée) everything about you, the good, the bad and the ugly. This is not an easy thing to do because you will be very vulnerable.

This is scary because we have always shown our best side to impress the person that we are interested in building a relationship with. Dating is where you can perform for your lover to impress them, but in marriage the real you will be revealed sooner or later. We must acknowledge who we really are. People will not change what they do not acknowledge. You must own your stuff. If you do not own your behavior, you will not change it. Whatever you defend, you will hold on to. In any process of rehabilitation, acknowledgement and admission are the first step. Each person must be open and honest about who they are. If alcohol abuse is the issue, a 12- step program encourages individuals to first admit that they have an alcohol problem. If drug abuse is the issue, the drug addict must first admit they have a drug addiction. If sin is the issue, the sinner must first admit that he or she has sinned. Individuals must know what is in them, and what they are capable of, so that they can deal properly with their relationship.

They should make a list of their baggage and their spouse's baggage and keep it handy for when they need it. For this to work, there must be a true admission of the baggage. It is totally essential for all healthy relationships, especially marriages. As was stated in the earlier chapters, the woman was brought to Adam by God, and they were both naked. There were no hidden agendas; everything was exposed. Adam knew everything about Eve and vice versa. He knew her background and where she came from. She was bone of his bone, and flesh of his flesh. Most of the problems that humans face is because their soul is messed up. 2 Corinthians 10:4 and 5 gives the answer to the soul's problem. *"For the weapons of our warfare are not carnal, but mighty through God to the pulling down of strong hold casting down imaginations, and every high thing that exalt itself against the knowledge of God, and bringing into captivity every thought to the obedience of Christ."*

    The solution to the soul's issues (habits, beliefs, family traits and unresolved issues) is the tree of life, which is Jesus. The fruit of the tree of knowledge of good and evil exalts itself against the knowledge of God. Before the fruit was consumed by man his thoughts, will and emotions were in line with God. Communion in the cool of the day was great. There were no misunderstandings or issues. Man did not need the knowledge of good and evil, he had the knowledge of God. The knowledge of hate, jealousy, envy, strife, murder, etc., became the work of the flesh. The knowledge of sin is now in man. Sin is at work because the Bible says in Romans 3:26, "The wages of sin is death." Galatians 5:19-21 says, *"Now the works of the flesh are evident, which are: adultery, fornication, uncleanness, lewdness, 20 idolatry, sorcery, hatred, contentions, jealousies, outbursts of wrath, selfish ambitions, dissensions, heresies, 21 envy, murders,[b] drunkenness, revelries, and the like; of which I tell you beforehand, just as I also told you in time past, that those who practice such things will not inherit the kingdom of God."*

God told Adam that the day that he ate from the tree of knowledge of good and evil, he would surely die. The flesh (soul) craves for things that destroy it: having fun, a good time, drinking, using drugs and having multiple sex partners. God gave Adam dominion over everything, so he was God's assistant on the earth. God allowed Adam to name everything and everyone. When individuals receive the word of God and confess that Jesus is Lord and are born again, they gain again the knowledge of God. Yes, the tree of life! The knowledge of good and evil is brought under captivity to the obedience of Christ. The Word of God is spirit and life. Hebrew 11:1 says, *"Now faith is a well-grounded assurance of that for which we hope, and a conviction of the reality of things which we do not see."* Faith in the Word of God is that vehicle that restores the soul. The breath of God makes an individual, a living soul again. David says in Psalms 23 that, *"...He restored my soul."* Faith in anything gives the ability to go beyond physical and emotional obstacles. I plead, beg, and encourage you, PLEASE do not keep a list of every wrong thing your spouse does. If you must keep a check list, write every good thing that you see and know about your spouse and count your blessings – name them one by one. Give God the praise for every good thing that your spouse does for you because they didn't have to. Yes, even if it's their duty, they still don't have to do it. What if God kept a list on everything you do wrong? God looks beyond your faults and sees your need.

As Adam and Eve were naked, so must couples be, with nothing hidden. Adam knew her background and where she came from. Pour out your souls to one another.

Discussion

What is an encounter?
What doesn't my spouse know about me?

Chapter 14
Step 2: Submission

Encounter brings you to submission. The second step in handling the baggage in marriage is submission. Submission is moving under or beneath the mission. Submission is changing your position and understanding of your spouse. You must stand under them. Have you ever heard someone say, "walk a mile in my shoes"? In other words, they want you to empathize! Empathy is the ability to understand and share the feelings of another. Submission is a yielding of ones will (heart) to another. This gives you real power. Think about a swimmer; until he fully yields his thoughts, he will never have the power to rest and sleep on the water. One of the greatest miracles in the Bible, in my opinion, is walking on the water, and I realized the other day that we have the power to lay on the water and defy gravity and physics.

Proverbs 4:7 says that, *"Wisdom is the principal thing; therefore, get wisdom. And in all your getting, get understanding"*. Even, though wisdom is the principal thing, wisdom loses its power or impact without understanding. God demonstrated the second step in intimacy by submitting to the relationship of man. God came down to man, and lived as man, so that he could really understand man. Hebrews 4:15 *"For we do not have a High Priest who cannot sympathize with our weaknesses, but was in all points tempted as we are, yet without sin."* Ephesians 5:21 says, as it relates to a husband and wife that they should, *"submit one to another in the fear of God"*. First, they must know that their lives now must be lived with their spouse in mind, just like a Christian should live unto God, not themselves. Galatians 2:20 says that, *"I am crucified with Christ; nevertheless, I live; yet not I, but Christ liveth in me."*

Marriage involves two different people and different genders becoming one. The amazing thing about this is that God made the man and the woman to physically fit just fine. But the real issues come from the soul, their minds, will and emotions. Therefore, handling the baggage individuals have is a real issue. For example, there can be two children born to the same parents, raised up together, been reared in the same neighborhood, and attended the same school, but may turn out to be totally opposites. It is because of the tree of the knowledge of good and evil, that people have baggage in the first place. People can handle their baggage through the big "C" word. Yes, COMMUNICATION. It is totally essential for all healthy relationships, especially marriage.

Communication is the vehicle through which knowledge, information, desires, needs, wants, etc. are transferred between two parties. Knowledge is the sum or amount of what has been perceived, discovered or learned. Knowledge then births understanding. Understanding means to stand under someone, to support them, and to back them. If someone has an individual's support, they will have an open mind to any and everything that individual says, feels, or thinks. Having an open mind will allow them to receive more knowledge of each other. Understanding is when an individual change their position and begins to stand under their spouse. Their thinking become aligns with their spouse. Knowing one another's family traits, habits and beliefs will put them in position to be related to. Even if one of the spouses is wrong about what they are discussing, if the other spouse sees the discussion through their eyes, they have a good chance of being enlightened by them.

The position an individual take has a profound effect on their understanding. People must beware of "friendly fire" or they will be wounded or killed by someone who is on their side. One of the causes of "friendly fire" is someone who gets out of position and gets in the line of fire of the enemy. They must adjust their positions so that their spouse is not in the same line of fire with their enemy. When an individual position themselves, it affects their perspective. Their perspective affects their reception of a message and how they respond to the message. Yes, where an individual is, affects what they see. A clear example of this can happen is in a story of something that happened to me one day, when I was on my way home from work. I stopped at a traffic light, where I was the third car from the intersection. When the light changed to green, the traffic didn't move. I said to myself, "the driver in front of me must have fallen asleep. The light is green, let's go." Finally, the traffic began to move, and that's when I saw that the lead car was trying to make a right turn, but there was a person in a wheelchair who was crossing in the intersection. I immediately felt sick about my perspective. Because of the position of where I was, I couldn't see or understand why the driver of the lead car didn't move when the light changed to green, until I changed my position in the intersection to where the lead car was.

Communication has two components: a speaker and a listener. The speaker voices or expresses, and the listener hears and understands what was expressed to them. We were given two ears and one mouth which says to me, that we should listen twice as much as we speak. We should listen to understand so that we can respond properly to what was expressed to us. The speaker's goal should be to share their feelings or their thoughts without accusing, attacking, labeling and judging while expressing their feelings. The listener's goal is to provide safety, understanding and clarity, without agreeing, disagreeing, advising or defending while being calm enough to hear (Petersen, 2007). In relationships, a person will never understand what is being communicated until they have lined up. People must know the position they play with their spouse; they are not in front or behind, nor to the right or the left. They must stand in the same place, at the same time. In every situation, they must know that they are one with their spouse. They are on the same side. It is impossible to be one with another individual, and not be on same side. They must take this position no matter what.

Communication is not just made up of words exchanged between two people or more. Communication also occurs when the hearer receives the intended message from the speaker. Many times, the receiver interprets what the speaker is saying based upon their own baggage they carry. Yes, their habits, family traits and their beliefs. So, they never receive the intended message. Communication is hard work! It is a whole lot of giving and taking. Because the speaker is responsible for the intended message received by the hearer, he or she will have to make any necessary adjustments in their delivery to ensure that the intended message is received by the hearer. The hearer or receiver of the communication also has the responsibility of listening with an open mind and without assumptions. They should have no preconceived ideas of what the messenger is trying to say, and they should never use prior experience with a former lover to interpret what their spouse is saying. The listener should repeat back to the sender what they believe the sender was trying to say.

Relationships can only be established and sustained through good communication. God made us in His image, which means He had a relationship with Adam. He didn't wait for Adam to call, text, email or "holler" at Him. No, He came down in the cool of the day to commune with Adam. When Adam broke the connection and he could not text, email or "holler", God had to adjust the way He communicated with mankind. The Old Testament showed that He mostly dealt with one man at a time to speak to mankind (Noah, Abraham, and Moses, to name a few). He also added a letter, and the scroll to communicate with His people. Then, He began to use the prophets, judges, kings and priests to stay in touch with mankind. Because the message of love was not being received, God made another adjustment. After 42 generations He sent His son, Emmanuel, (which means God is with us) to live among mankind. Jesus paid the price that connected God's people, back to God. Because God wanted to get closer to His people, He sent His spirit to live in them. His example demonstrates that everyone in relationships should make the necessary adjustments to ensure the message of love is being communicated. They must adjust the way they have been carrying their baggage. God submitted himself to mankind, and came down in the flesh, to experience humanity. God learned how man felt to be hungry, sleepy, tired, and thirsty through Jesus' life on earth. Jesus also showed mankind how to become one with God through discipleship.

So, each person must submit to their spouse. They should change their position of being single and pleasing themselves. Seek now to please your fiancé (fiancée) more than yourself. 1 Corinthians 13:5 says, *"love seeketh not her own..."* Love seeks to please, not to be pleased. Married couples must understand that they are one, which means if their spouse loses, they both have lost. They should not try to make their spouse lose. Practice letting them win a disagreement in a way that, they as a couple, are better off because of it. Couples must know that they are not just on the same team, they are the same player. Yes, the two are one. Everyone else is their opponent. Genesis 2:6 tells us we are, *"Bone of my bone, and flesh of my flesh..."*

Understanding each other's family traits, habits, beliefs and unresolved issues is fine and good, but if each spouse's needs are not met, frustration will be the result. This frustration could end in separation and divorce. Therefore, after understanding your spouse's family traits, beliefs, habits and unresolved issues, they must understand what their spouse's needs are.

God ordained marriage and he had a plan for success in marriage. The key is understanding the roles and the needs of each other. The failure of a marriage and relationship is mostly due to the misunderstanding of the roles, and needs not being met by the spouse, thus opening the door for the spouse to be tempted to get those needs met outside the marriage. The roles are different, and they are necessary. Each gender is built to perform their role. The male is the protector, planter and the caretaker, and that is the reason why he is called the husband to the wife. The male is a planter because he has seeds. He is designed as the gardener who takes care of the garden. The female is the help-mate or the para-cleat and the encourager. The female is the multiplier and a producer. Whatever the male gives her, she will incubate it and give it back to the male, greater than what he has given her. The roles tie into the needs of each spouse. The male provides the seed to the female through sex, and she receives the seed and incubates it for nine months to give the man a child. God told Adam to be fruitful and multiply and the male cannot fulfill this assignment without the female.

A need is different than a want. A need is what helps you to function. The male needs the following four things from their spouse:

1. SEX: *(Intercourse)* He does not want sex, but he needs sex. He needs his wife to make sex available to him without reservation.
2. RESPECT: (Honored) He does not want respect, but he needs it. He needs his wife to praise him and hold him in high regard.
3. AN ATTRACTIVE SPOUSE: (Presentable) He needs his spouse to look beautiful always.
4. DOMESTIC SUPPORT: (Comforter) He needs his home to be a safe place. He needs a place of peace and comfort from all the stress of the outside. Home needs to be a safe place, free from drama, and negativity.

The female needs the following four things from their spouse:

1. AFFECTION: (Love) She may want sex, but she does not need sex. She needs affection, such as telling her that you love her, holding hands, receiving flowers and cards, doors to be opened, to be a priority and date nights.
2. CONVERSATION: (Listening) She needs her spouse to talk to her and listen attentively; again, she does not want this she needs it.
3. HONESTY & OPENESS (Confide In Her) She needs her spouse to tell her everything.
4. FINANCIAL SECURITY (Worry Free). She shouldn't have to worry about money issues. She needs her own funds to buy herself things that makes her feel pretty and cute. (Myles Munroe Ministries).

If everyone knows their roles and executes it, they will have a successful relationship and marriage. If everyone understands their spouse's needs and meets them, they will have a successful marriage. *(Please purchase Dr. Myles Munroe book on Relationships, because it is a must read!)* Misunderstandings brew conflicts and chaos.

Stephen A. Butterfield, Sr.

When the weather is foggy, we say that there is a mist and you cannot see clearly, well, when we remove the "m-i-s-" from understanding, we can see clearly.

Tip

The knowledge that men are different from women is shown is an example when a wife can submit and understand her husband. Many wives get frustrated that their husband does not express his concern and care. You, the wife know that something is bothering him and, something is on his mind, but instead of talking to you about it, he just walks around the house not saying anything. In your frustration, you add to this problem by nagging. Yes, I did say nag. In addition to what is already bothering him, now he is in a full-blown argument with you, for no reason.

Can we get some understanding before we get into an argument? Most boys grow up, learning that when they fall, fail, or get hurt, everyone tells them to *"suck it up, get up and be a man"*. Most men are taught not to dwell and think about hurt, pain, problems and failures. So, all they are hearing is, *"suck it up, and be a man"*. So, as a man, the last person you want to hear those words from is your wife. So instead of sharing his concerns, he feels that he must be a man and figure it out. Some wives have made those same statements, "You're the man, you figure it out".

Can I share something else with you ladies, that may help your husband to open to you in the future? When you detect that your husband is concerned about things that he is not sharing with you, the worst thing you can do is to force him to speak to you about it. Here is my recommendation. When you detect this, use a lot of patience and simply tell your husband that you know something is bothering him, that you are there for him, and that you know that he is well and able. Typically, after ten times of this assurance, the husband will begin to open slowly. Show the support and be that help-mate that you have been designed to be.

Discussion

What is submission?
Do you understand your spouse's family traits,
habits, beliefs, unresolved issues and needs?
Which of the above listed items does your spouse
seems not to understand about you?

Chapter 15
Step 3: Transformation

Submission brings on transformation. However, this is a process which happens over time. METAMORPHISIS is the process of transformation of an immature form to an adult form, in a more distinct stage. Giving up on your single mindedness and yielding to your fiancé (fiancée) and their needs and desires. Your perspective and perception are based on the change of position you made in submission. Marriage demands change. If an individual does not intend on changing when they get married, they should do themselves and the poor soul they intend on marrying a favor and stay single.

People must change their ways, thinking, and habits. God's love is unconditional, but His love has conditions. He loves individuals just as they are and loves them too much to let them stay that way. God's love demands a change in people. Individuals must have personal Bible study, attend Bible study and Sunday School in order to learn what it is going to take to develop a sound relationship with God. Then, they must seek to make the necessary changes. Paul in one of his letters to the church says that, "*...we must die daily.*" An individual must be conformed to the image of God's son, Jesus. He also says in Romans 12 in verse 2, "*And be not conformed this world; but be ye transformed by the renewing of your mind...*" Matthew 19:8 says, "*And he saith unto them, Moses because of the hardness of your hearts suffered you to put away your wives:*" This takes some work and commitment. If individuals were practicing this as Christians, it would be easier to lay down their thinking and begin to think about what it is to build and secure their relationship with their spouse.

As you understand each other better day by day, you can sometimes know what each other is about to say. Sometimes my wife and I look at something, and we have the same reaction because we are cleaving and becoming one.

The single mind set must be changed into a marriage mind set. You don't look to and for yourself, but for your marriage. Your marriage is your first ministry. Your thinking must now be how we accomplish the vision for this marriage, and this family. There is a mandate on each family; the man must have the vision from God, and the woman is his help-mate. She is equipped to help the man to fulfil his mandate. Now, the focus is not on the individual in the marriage, but the marriage and its assignment on the earth. Therefore, instead of trying to win a discussion, each person is trying to see what is going to benefit the marriage and its vision.

Let us take a look at the caterpillar's transformation to a butterfly. The caterpillar takes what it eats, regurgitates it and forms a cocoon, which covers it from head to toe. In the cocoon is where the transformation happens. When the transformation is complete, the butterfly has to break itself out of the cocoon, which gives their wings strength. The butterfly would then leave the cocoon behind. As it relates to transformation in marriage, each spouse must take the knowledge of their spouse's family traits, habits, beliefs, unresolved issues and needs and submerge themselves into their spouse. They absorb everything about their spouse; yes, they take it all in. This action changes each spouse's perspective of their spouse and they begin to see their spouse differently, just like the caterpillar's low point of view changes as the butterfly flies with a higher point of view.

Proverbs 23:7(a) *"For as he thinketh in his heart, so is he."* Whatever you meditate on, that is what you will become. So, don't meditate on the family traits, beliefs, habits, and unresolved issues, but on the needs of your spouse, and you will become that. *"A man is literally what he thinks, his character being the complete sum of all his thoughts"* (James Allen).

Discussion

What is transformation?
What have you changed?
How often do you think about your spouse?

Chapter 16
Step 4: Oneness

"Male and female created he them and blessed them, and called their name Adam, in the day when they were created." - Genesis 5:2

They were created two in one; but because Adam was lonely, God took Eve out of Adam and made two. God then said that a man should leave his father and mother and cleave to his wife, and they shall be one flesh.

Intimacy makes couples one. Consummation plays a key part in the oneness. The cleaving of the spirit is based on the encounter, submission and transformation which brings "oneness". When oneness becomes a reality, more couples reveal themselves, seek to understand their spouse, and think as a married person.

Oneness is when a couple can complete their spouse's sentences, and when they see something, they can tell when their spouse thinks about it. Oneness is being what is needed to make the family whole and complete. Your destiny and purpose are linked together.

I truly believe that this is the purpose of marriage – couples working together to fulfil their purpose and assignment on the earth.

Marriage the Journey

Discussion

*Do you feel" in sync" with your spouse?
Do you feel that you can almost finish their sentence?
Do people ever say that you guys look alike?*

Stephen A. Butterfield, Sr.

Part 8
Annual Marital
Check-Up

Chapter 17
Annual Marital Check-Up

The Annual Marital Check Up is like getting an annual physical with your physician. You get your blood pressure, heart rate, temperature and vital signs checked. Attend a marriage workshop or conference and invest in some books on marriage and relationship. Read them, and then discuss what you all glean from them and see how it can enhance your marriage.

Check the eight "C"s in your marriage. Check your family traits and see if it has a positive or negative affect on your marriage. Check to see if you are satisfying each other's love languages and see whether it changed. Check your habits and see if some good habits were practiced, and bad habits were dropped.

Check to see if you all still have shared goals and values. Check to see if your heart is still pure toward each other. Check your commitment to each other. Revisit the baggage list and see if there are any changes. Revisit the things that you used to like, to see if you still like them. Remember that desires, likes and dislikes change from time to time, so you must revisit those desires, likes and dislikes to ensure that each spouse stays relevant. Couples should be prepared to unpack, and re-pack at different intervals in their marriage.

Marriage the Journey

Discussion

*When was your last marital checkup?
What did you learn that surprised you?
Have you scheduled the next marital checkup?*

References

McGoldrick, M., Gerson, R., & Petry, S. (2008). *Genograms: Assessment and intervention* (3rd ed.). New York, NY: WW Norton & Co.

Chapman, G. (202011). The 5 Love Languages: *The Secret to Love That Lasts*. Chicago, IL: Northfield

Petersen, P. C. (2007). *Why Don't We Listen Better: Communicating & Connecting in Relationships*. Portland, OR: Petersen.

Smith-Holmes, R., (2016). *A Word on Love* (2th ed.). Atlanta, GA: MEWE.

http://www.marketwatch.com/story/5-habits-of-the-very-best-investors-2014-03-12
    Richard Buck contributed to this article.

Feldman, R. (2011). *Development Across the Life Span* (6th ed.). Upper Saddle River, NJ:Pearson.

About the Author

Stephen A. Butterfield

Born April 10, 1956 in Nassau N.P. Bahamas to Jack and Pearl Butterfield. Stephen was the youngest of four children and is the father of six adult children, 16 grandchildren, and one great grandson. He is married to Ann Pearl Butterfield. He was ordained Pastor of Outreach by Light of the World International Association in 2010 and ordained an Elder there by Light of the World

Christian Tabernacle (LOTW) in 2005. He is involved with many ministries at LOTW including Outreach Ministry, Divorce Care Ministry, Worship Arts, Hospital Chaplaincy, Rockdale Hospital, Conyers, Ga., Traditional Nursing Home, Lithonia, Ga., Light House ministry, and Director of the Ministers. He holds a Bachelor of Arts degree in accounting from FMU with a GPA of 3.33 and received his Master of Business Administration from the University of Phoenix in 2010. Master of Psychology Counseling-Children and Family in 2014.

Highlights, Awards, Honors & Accomplishments:

Stephen played the trumpet as a member of his high school band. He leads the gospel group, Flamingo Singers, from the time he was 12 years old to 20, He served as the youth pastor for 17 years and choir director for 20 years at the House of God Miracle Temple in W. Hollywood, FL. He was a member of the 500 Role Models of Dade County Public Schools; deputy of juvenile justice in Florida; and coached basketball, football and baseball for 15 years (Scott Lake Vikings). Wrote and song a great worship song "We worship you", "There is Hope", "Here I am", "Call on the Savior" and "Too Late."

Stephen A. Butterfield, Sr.

Contact Information:

For appearances and upcoming event information, please contact Butterfield's Ministries at: 770-906-0607 or:

www.butterfieldsministriesworldwide.com

Email   annpbutterfield@yahoo.com

www.ingramcontent.com/pod-product-compliance
Lightning Source LLC
LaVergne TN
LVHW041625070426
835507LV00008B/462